501 IMAGES OF
TAJ MAHAL
AND GLIMPSES OF MUGHAL AGRA

Reprinted 2005
Published in 2004 by
Prakash Books India Pvt. Ltd.
1, Ansari Road, Darya Ganj,
New Delhi - 110 002
Ph.: (011) 2324 3050, Fax: (011) 2324 6975
E-mail: sales@prakashbooks.com
Website: www.prakashbooks.com

Editor: Monisha Mukundan
Introduction: Late Keshav Dev Sharma
Research and concept: Reeta Khullar
Photographs on pages: 31-32, 33
Courtesy: Ashok Prabhakar Mote.

ISBN 81-7234-081-8
Cover processed, scanned by: Radiant Graphics (Pvt.) Ltd.
E-mail: radiant_graphics2001@yahoo.com
Printed and bound at Ajanta Offset & Packaging, New Delhi

501 IMAGES OF
TAJ MAHAL
AND GLIMPSES OF MUGHAL AGRA
PRAKASH
BOOKS

INTRODUCTION

More than any other building or indeed any other image, the Taj Mahal symbolises India to people all over the world. This tomb, built in the seventeenth century by a grieving Mughal emperor for his wife, has become the focus of innumerable romantic stories, of colourful fantasies. It has fascinated artists and photographers, connoisseurs of beauty and poets, travellers and dreamers ever since it was built.

Each visitor to this remarkable monument takes away a uniquely personal impression of the Taj. The marble of which it is built changes as the sunlight waxes and wanes through the day and takes on a special, insubstantial, dream quality by moonlight. Each season brings its own subtle variations and the clouds in the sky above create a quicksilver play of illumination and shadow during the monsoon.

In many ways, the changing face of the Taj and all the varied architectural and artistic elements that contribute to its monumental presence characterize the period of the great Mughals. The Taj epitomises the artistic inheritance of the Mughal emperor Shah Jahan, the fifth of his line, who built this extraordinary structure.

Shah Jahan, the fifth Mughal emperor, came to the throne at a time when the empire was already well established. He inherited a stable throne, a developed administrative system and a prosperous treasury. Shah Jahan had been groomed to be emperor, spending his childhood at court, absorbing all the imperial and artistic achievements of his father and grandfather. A tradition of courtly life dictated the pattern of his daily routine. Going to war was part of the Mughal style but so was a refined and elegant appreciation of beauty and the finer things of life. From his ancestors, Shah Jahan inherited both the skills of a warrior and the love of beauty in all its forms.

Babur, the first of the Mughal rulers, came from Central Asia. Babur's ancestors included Timur, or Tamerlane, who had swept into India in 1398, leaving a trail of plunder and destruction in his wake. On his mother's side, Babur was descended from Chinghiz Khan. He inherited the throne of Ferghana in modern-day Uzbegistan when he was only eleven years old. It is said that Babur first learnt of India in the city of Samarkand and resolved to conquer "the land of the Ganges". He ruled from Kabul for a time, from where he made four unsuccessful attempts to invade India. He finally succeeded in 1526, defeating the last of the Lodi Sultans at the Battle of Panipat. He proclaimed himself king but had to fight to secure his position. Babur ruled India for only four years, and therefore had little opportunity to build anything permanent. In the midst of wars, Babur nevertheless had the time to write a journal in fascinating detail, and to plant gardens and orchards that reminded him of his home in Kabul. His love of gardens, his curiosity and interest in nature were to come to fruition in the lives and work of his descendants, including Shah Jahan.

Babur's son Humayun lost the kingdom for a time and then regained it during a period of constant struggle and intermittent warfare. He established his capital in present-day Delhi and built a fort here, which was taken over by his foe Sher Shah who ruled for a time. However, Humayun did undertake some architectural projects, setting up a tradition of building that was to be enlarged and given character by his son Akbar.

Akbar, who came to the throne when he was thirteen years old, consolidated his father's military gains and went on to defeat his enemies through a mixture of conquest and diplomacy. He absorbed the ways of his people and created a style of architecture that amalgamated Indian traditions with the Central Asian legacy that his father and grandfather had brought with them. At Agra Fort and at his new town of Fatehpur Sikri, Akbar used red sandstone and marble to create a new architectural vocabulary that reflected his eclectic interests. He is also thought by some scholars to have been involved with the building of Humayun's tomb in Delhi. Humayun's tomb is seen by many as the precursor to the Taj. All the elements that define the Taj are already apparent in Humayun's tomb. Here we have a tomb raised on a high plinth surmounted by a dome of splendid proportions. The edifice is set like a jewel in the centre of a 'char-bagh' garden, a garden divided into four sections in a very formal and mathematically exact form. All these components were to be refined and perfected in the tomb that Shah Jahan built for his beloved Empress, perhaps the first major monument to an empress, rather than the emperor himself, in Mughal times.

Shah Jahan spent his childhood at his grandfather's court and would have been aware of Emperor Akbar's involvement with all the buildings that he was creating, especially at the new city of Fatehpur Sikri. Akbar's lively curiosity and his interest in music, literature, art and architecture would have nurtured an atmosphere of learning and aesthetic appreciation. By this time, the growing power and prosperity of the Mughal empire made the court a place where grand projects were envisaged and carried out, where cities could be built on an emperor's command. It became a magnet for talented people of every sort, where skill and creativity earned fabulous rewards. The might of the great Mughals was matched by their patronage of the arts and of skilled craftsmanship of every kind

Emperor Jahangir, Shah Jahan's father, took a keen interest in painting as well as the other arts. He was a renowned connoisseur of precious stones and like his forefathers, he loved beautiful things. The delicacy of fine detail in painting, the awareness of natural beauty, of flowers and plants and nature were all to play a part in the final design of the Taj. For, as much as grandly conceived architecture, what sets the Taj apart from any other building in the world is the attention which has been paid to the decoration of its surfaces, to the pietra dura and the marble screens and the representations of flowers and creepers, leaves and plants in sculpture, inlay and paintings.

The court in which Shah Jahan grew up was one in which wealth and the appreciation of beauty marched hand-in-hand with power and military prowess. He was trained in the arts of war and in the pleasures of peace. Like other princes at the Mughal court, he participated in sports and hunting expeditions. His appreciation of architecture was complemented by his passion for gems, an interest that he shared with his father. His knowledge of precious stones led to an interest in designing their setting and he is said to have developed both a connoisseur's eye and a skilled hand in working with gems. The use of precious stones was not confined to jewellery in the Mughal court. Arms and armaments were often beautifully decorated and studded with stones. Sometimes boxes and wine bowls were also finely adorned, as were hookah bases and other accoutrements of a royal lifestyle. Shah Jahan would have been surrounded by bejewelled objects and his love of gems was also to play a part in his masterpiece, the Taj Mahal.

In fact, it is said to be his love of precious stones that led to his meeting with Mumtaz Mahal.The story goes that a meena bazaar, a sort of small fair, was arranged at the palace, to celebrate the new year. Royal princesses and noblewomen took stalls and offered trinkets for sale, creating a colourful evening's entertainment for the royal family and favoured courtiers. Among the young girls who participated in the fair was the niece of Empress Nur Jahan. Her name was Arjumand Bano Begum. Shah Jahan, who was then known as Prince Khurram, came to the fair. His interest was caught by the gems that Arjumand Bano offered at her stall. Pausing to buy them, he fell in love with the beautiful keeper of the stall and married her.

There is no historical basis to this charming story. However it is perfectly possible that it might have happened this way. What we do know is that the marriage of Prince Khurram was arranged to Arjumand Bano Begum, the niece of Empress Nur Jahan. The young couple had to wait for four years before they were permitted to marry. Jahangir himself attended the wedding and is said to have been very fond of his daughter-in-law. It was he who bestowed upon her the title of Mumtaz Mahal, the 'Exalted one of the Palace".

For Prince Khurram, his wedding was the beginning of a devoted relationship that was to last for the nineteen years of their married life. Despite an extensive harem and his other wives, he is said to have cared only for Mumtaz Mahal. He never had children by any other woman. Mumtaz Mahal in turn was utterly devoted to her husband. She travelled with him wherever he went and was his closest advisor and confidante. Through all the ups and downs of military campaigns and all the machinations of political intrigue, she remained steadfast and supportive.

In the nineteen years of their marriage, Mumtaz Mahal had fourteen children, of which only seven survived. She accompanied her husband despite pregnancies, and childbirth in the field, coping with all the rigours of life in an armed camp no matter what condition she was in. A great deal of this period would have spent in tented camps, as Shah Jahan was engaged in military campaigns to consolidate the empire. He was sent to subdue recalcitrant rulers in Rajasthan and in the south, travelling arduous distances despite the luxuries that an imperial camp would undoubtedly have provided. And, wherever he went, Mumtaz Mahal went with him.

There was no clear line of succession in the Mughal dynasty, with the result that Mughal princes were constantly embroiled in intrigues and conspiracies against each other and against their father. Prince Khurram was a favourite of his father's but he had to be constantly on guard in the highly charged political atmosphere of the Mughal court. In such a situation, it was hard to trust anyone. In Mumtaz Mahal, Prince Khurram found a wholehearted and utterly loyal partner. He grew to depend on her a great deal.

Although Mumtaz Mahal was the niece of Nur Jahan, Jahangir's Empress, and Nur Jahan had initially supported Prince Khurram, the situation changed with Jahangir's growing ill-health. Nur Jahan began to take an increasingly important role in the affairs of state and as her power grew, she withdrew her support from Prince Khurram, favouring another prince in the burgeoning struggle for the throne. Prince Khurram, however, had the backing of his father-in-law, a powerful noble at the court, who also happened to be Nur Jahan's brother.

As Emperor Jahangir's health failed, and the struggle for succession developed, Prince Khurram went into open rebellion. Accompanied by Mumtaz Mahal and a band of followers, he fled from Agra. Jahangir, ailing and under the influence of Nur Jahan, sent the imperial troops in pursuit.Prince Khurram and his followers had to evade their pursuers, and were harried from place to place.

When news came of Jahangir's death in 1627, Prince Khurram hastened towards Agra. His father-in-law, who was at the court, moved decisively to divest Nur Jahan of power and to rally support for Prince Khurram. In the conflict and intrigue that followed, the other claimants to the throne were put to death to clear the way for Prince Khurram, as was the pattern in Mughal times. Each succession was accompanied by bloodshed and the death of rival claimants and this was no exception. Prince Khurram entered the city of Agra in a triumphant procession in January 1628.

He came to the throne as Emperor Shah Jahan, which means Ruler of the World, a title bestowed on him earlier by Jahangir, after a victorious campaign. When he became Emperor in 1618, it seemed as if Shah Jahan had everything anyone could desire. An empire at peace. A fabulous court, wealth beyond counting, heirs to ensure the continuity of his line and an Empress who shared his dreams and appreciation of beauty.

It lasted for a scant three years. In 1631, while accompanying her husband, as she had always done, this time on a campaign to Burhanpur in the Deccan, Empress Mumtaz Mahal went into labour with her fourteenth child. It was a difficult labour. While an anxious Shah Jahan waited and the entire camp held its collective breath, Mumtaz Mahal struggled to deliver her child. It soon became apparent that something was catastrophically wrong.

It is said that when the Empress realised that she was going to die, she called Shah Jahan to her side and made him promise her two things. He would not have children by any other woman and, he would build her a tomb that the world would never forget.

Her death devastated Shah Jahan. Contemporary chroniclers, notably historian Abdul Hamid Lahori, the author of the *Badshahnama* which is the official history of Shah Jahan's reign, record the fact that his beard turned white overnight. He went into mourning for over two years, refusing to eat anything but the plainest food, banning music and dance and all the pleasures he had once enjoyed, grieving inconsolably for his beloved wife.

When he emerged from the pall of darkness and seclusion into which he had slipped at her death, he turned at once to fulfilling the promise he had made Mumtaz Mahal. He would build her a tomb that would stun the world.

From the royal apartments on the ramparts of the Agra Fort, there is a view of the languidly flowing Yamuna River. It curves away from the fort in a great sweep that glows like molten gold at sunset.

Within the curve of the river, cradled by the water, was a stretch of vacant land. It belonged to Raja Man Singh, a Rajput noble. The Emperor offered the nobleman a generous exchange, giving him a sumptuous mansion in place of the land. The agreement was finalised and the site set for the garden tomb the Emperor planned to build.

The foundation of Shah Jahan's involvement with architecture and his career as the great builder of the Mughal period, came with the making of this tomb. For he flung himself into the planning and design, taking a keen interest in the minutest detail. He brought to bear upon it his passion for gems and decorative arts as well as a highly developed aesthetic sense, nurtured by the years he had spent at the courts of his grandfather and his father. All his talent, all his knowledge was focussed on the project that absorbed him and consoled him in the years following Mumtaz Mahal's death.

Immediately after her death, Mumtaz Mahal had been buried in Burhanpur, in a temporary tomb until Shah Jahan found a place for her monument. Now the Empress' body was transported from Burhanpur in south India to Agra, where she was laid in another hurriedly built grave until her final resting place was prepared for her. It was to take twenty-two years.

There is a great deal of disagreement amongst historians about who designed the Taj Mahal. What seems clear, however, is that it was the logical successor to a style of garden tomb that had already been explored with the building of Humayun's tomb in Delhi. As his son, Akbar would have had a hand in the design of Humayun's tomb. That influence found an echo in his grandson's tribute to Mumtaz Mahal. The square, raised plinth, the garden setting, the monumental dome; these elements were already part of the Mughal style. What distinguished Shah Jahan's masterpiece was the harmonious way in which he combined these architectural elements with his own awareness of the decorative arts, and with a sense of proportion so exquisite that the result seems perfection itself.

It is believed that twenty thousand workers laboured for almost two decades to bring Shah Jahan's vision of perfection to life in stone. Masons, artists, labourers, carpenters, jewellers, inlay workers, sculptors, mathematicians, draftsmen,bricklayers, engineers, all came to live beside the Jamuna River. They came from distant parts of the empire to settle in the imperial capital, bringing their families with them. A small settlement sprang up beside the site. Gradually it grew into a permanent residential area. Families moved in. Children were born here and grew to adulthood in the shadow of the construction site, where the sound of hammer on stone rang continuously all through the day. At one point, a ten-mile-long ramp was constructed to transport materials to the construction site.

The details of managing a project of such vast scope are mind-boggling. Raw materials had to be procured from the deserts of Rajasthan and from places as far away as Persia and Afghanistan, Burma and Kashgar, and carried to Agra. There was marble from the mines at Makrana, beyond Jodhpur, there was yellow amber from Burma, lapis lazuli from Afghanistan, jade from China, and other stones such as coral, chalcedony, green beryl, jasper, amethyst, agate and onyx from various regions of India. All this marble and the semi-precious stones would have had to be checked for quality and then stored and guarded until they were required. A regular check would have had to be maintained on their quantity and use, so that the supply kept pace with the consumption. Accounts had to be prepared and maintained. The work of skilled craftsmen of many different guilds had to be coordinated. Managing the workforce and the needs of so many varied artisans and workers would have required organizational skills of an extremely high order.

Water from the Yamuna was used for the construction. But that same river had to guarded against as the foundations were being laid. The annual flooding had to be taken into consideration, the site on the riverbank had to allow for the specific quality of the soil and the varying intensities of dampness that the river created. Experts of various sorts had to pool their knowledge and their resources to create ways of dealing with the problems that arose.

Shah Jahan was obsessed with the project. He took a personal interest in every detail and may even, according to some sources, have been involved in the design itself. Turning away from statecraft and the demands of the court, Shah Jahan put his energy into building his wife's tomb. From the royal apartments at the fort, he watched the construction progress on the skyline, keeping a close check on every aspect of its planning and implementation.

All his interest in architecture and the decorative arts came into play as the tomb developed. Craftsmen worked the marble surfaces until they resembled a piece of jewellery, incising and inlaying, carving shallow relief motifs. Traditional geometric patterns and innovative floral images were used to offset one another, creating arresting and beautiful visual juxtapositions that continue to fascinate visitors to this day. Intricately worked surfaces were set against plain areas so that the workmanship showed in an effective manner. Each detail was meticulously planned and each portion of the decoration was placed in harmony with the other elements of the whole. The Taj is never boring. There is always something new to discover, no matter how often you visit the monument. It is this quality that gives it such an enduring allure.

The mausoleum was finally completed in 1643, and on her birth anniversary, the body of Mumtaz Mahal was interred for the last time in the crypt below the main chamber of the Taj. Prayers were said and devotional music played as the Emperor bade a final farewell to his beloved wife, returning to the Fort by boat, as he had arrived.

In Mughal times, that was the preferred route to the Taj Mahal. The Emperor himself always travelled to the monument by boat, alighting at the fort and gradually approaching the tomb along the river.

The people would have used the gate we use today, entering the complex from the bazaar and the city, and approaching through the garden. The city must have been strung out along the river, beginning at the fort. So the people of the city would have been very aware of the river, of their monarch travelling down the Yamuna from his palace in the fort.

Today, visitors only become aware of the river towards the end of their exploration of the Taj. The twentieth century entrance is the one used by the common people during Mughal times, on the side away from the river. Arriving at the Taj through the city, visitors enter through a monumental gateway and approach the Taj through its char-bagh garden, designed in a formal, geometrically laid out pattern. The garden is a symbolic representation of ' a garden of paradise' and the pool in which the Taj is reflected so beautifully symbolises celestial abundance. Geometrically precise gardens such as this one were a feature of Mughal architecture and may be seen at Humayun's tomb and other mausoleums.

The main gate to the Taj Mahal is made of red sandstone, inlaid with marble. Its sheer size commands the attention of visitors, for it is carefully proportioned and adorned with beautiful calligraphy. The skill of the calligraphers and the designers is evident in the way they placed verses from the Koran in such perfect proportion that they seem to be of one size despite the changing perspective of the areas in which they are located, such as the monumental entrance gateway. The letters of the inscriptions create a sense of uniformity because the calligrapher took recourse to a simple device of optical illusion. The letters have been inscribed densely at the bottom with little plain surface between them; the inscription becomes more and more sparse as it rises, with more plain surface between the individual letters. Visually, the mathematical precision creates a sense of perfect harmony that soothes and elevates. There was a tradition at that time that artists remained anonymous, seldom signing their work. However, Amanat Khan, the chief calligrapher of the Taj Mahal already had a well-established reputation. He was responsible for the calligraphy work at Akbar's tomb at Sikandra and at the Madrasa Shahi mosque at Agra. As a privileged person, he was able to sign his work and date it, inside the calligraphic inscription on the left side of the southern iwan. That is why Amanat Khan's contribution to the calligraphy at the Taj is not doubted at all.

The beauty of the calligraphic inscription on the gateway to the Taj adds to its sense of dignified grandeur. It establishes a frame to the central structure. Rising to a height of about thirty metres, the gate acts as a prelude to the monumentality of the Taj itself, setting the stage, so to speak, for the massive yet fragile structure that confronts visitors as they emerge from the gateway.

Seen across the length of the garden, one's first view of the Taj is utterly arresting. Visitors walk as if entranced towards the tomb. Very few are prepared for its contradictory grandeur and fragile delicacy. For the structure rises to a height of over 74 metres up to the finial. The height exceeds the width by more than 17 metres, which creates the impression of a building soaring skywards. There is a sense of a delicately anchored bubble straining to break free. The square plinth seems to hold the dome in place, rooting it to the earth.

At the four corners of the plinth are slim tapering minarets which lead the eye upwards towards the central dome, creating a frame for the entire structure. The minarets bring about a harmony, creating a setting for the main dome in much the same way as the garden provides a setting for the entire structure.

The dome is actually a double dome. This structural device provided a suitable and proportionate ceiling to the mortuary chamber while allowing the outer shell to rise majestically into the sky. The idea of the double dome was used at Humayun's Tomb. At the Taj, the proportions have been perfected to create a gracefully elegant balance.

Flanking the soaring dome are four chattris or pavilions which provide visual support, clustering close to its base like smaller pinnacles encircling a peak. Every structural element supports and complements the sense of forms rising skywards, lifting the eye and the spirit to the heavens.

Under the sheltering dome is the main mortuary chamber, the heart of the entire edifice. Although the actual tombs are in a crypt below, at ground level the cenotaphs in the mortuary chamber provide a focus for the building. Mumtaz Mahal's cenotaph lies in the centre of the chamber, with Shah Jahan's beside her, on the right, as he was buried at his death in 1666. Both are decorated in exquisitely fine pietra dura work, like a pair of jewelled caskets. Originally, a gold railing encircled Mumtaz Mahal's cenotaph, but this was later replaced with one in marble.

The inlay work on the cenotaphs and the marble screen, and on the walls and borders of the building are intricately beautiful. In one place, forty-eight tiny pieces of multicoloured semi-precious stone have been used to create a single flower. The gems used for the decoration of the Taj Mahal came from all over India and from other countries as well.

The crypt below, in which the actual graves are located, was not always open to the public. It was a quiet place for prayer, to which only a few people came, making offerings of sheets for the graves or perfume in memory of the Empress. The floor was once covered with carpets and the graves with finely worked cloth. In contrast to the opulence above, it continues to be a softly lit, silent chamber, to which visitors go in a reverent, silent mood. Prayers are recited over the graves and incense lit. Fragrant flowers are offered here in memory of the long dead Empress and in memory of an Emperor's grief.

From the dim, spiritual atmosphere of the crypt, visitors re-enter the material world above ground as they return to the platform that surrounds the main chamber and are confronted by its purity of form and decoration once again. A significant part of the Taj's beauty is ascribed to the remarkable inlay work and calligraphy which covers the surface of the building. The fine inlay motifs create a sense of delicacy that is supplemented by the graceful screens and the panels of calligraphy.

The hall in which the cenotaphs lie is 24.35 metres in height. Sounds are echoed and magnified in this space, floating and soaring in a long undulation which fades so slowly that one seems to hear it even after it has fallen silent. The arrangement of the rooms and passages around the chamber are double-storeyed, identically arranged on both floors. There are four rectangular rooms on the four sides, with octagonal rooms at the corners, interconnected to one another. Except for the entrance on the south facade the other sides are enclosed with screens divided into tiny compartments filled with glass. The tiny glass panes are slightly translucent so that they filter the light. Only very subdued light reaches the central chamber, bathing the cenotaphs in a soft, delicate glow. The glare of the marble outside is tempered by the gentle lighting within, a contrast that creates an atmosphere of solemnity, quietening even modern-day visitors with its meditative quality.

Each of the four facades of the tomb is composed of a grand iwan or arched entrance. The iwan is flanked on either side by small double arches one on top of the other. They are rectangular while the arched alcoves of equal size at the angled corners of the tomb are semi-octagonal. The care with which the architect conceived of all the details is evident in the way that the rectangular alcoves are distinctly visible from afar but the ones on the sides had to be semi-octagonal if they were to be seen in perspective. Each section of the facade is demarcated on both sides by attached pilasters which rise from the plinth in a chevron pattern inlaid in the marble. Each pilaster is surmounted by a beautiful pinnacle of lotus buds and finials, which ornament the superstructure.

Each of these architectural features provides a 'canvas' to the artists who adorned the Taj with relief carvings and inlay. All the ornamentation is either geometric or floral, each one complementing the other with extraordinary felicity. Lilies and narcissi, tulips and irises, grace the curves the plaques, the arches and the doorways. Flowers were a part of the Mughal court, filling gardens with their fragrance, providing bouquets and perfumes for the harems.It was perhaps inevitable that flowers would be the major decorative feature in so Mughal a monument.

Flower motifs have been sculpted, incised, and used in inlays, glazed and tiled enamelling, mosaic, stucco and painting, on interior and exterior surfaces.

The marble dados are an exceptionally gorgeous feature of the Taj. They follow the pattern of miniature paintings that began during Jahangir's reign. In the studies of flowers and animals that Jahangir commissioned, the artists added a border of exquisite beauty. Painters who specialised in borders worked almost independently of the miniature painters, so that the border itself became a separate work of art. The borders often featured leaf and floral patterns from Persian miniatures. Chinese cloud-forms sometimes appeared in the background. Such miniatures evidently inspired the architects of the Taj and artisans translated them into stone, adapting all the motifs, including the cloud-forms, which have been used in particular profusion at the Agra Fort as well.The inlay borders used on the Taj mark a stage of perfection. Each dado is presented like a beautiful Mughal painting, with exquisitely graceful forms.

The two red sandstone buildings on either side of the structure enhance the symmetry which characterizes the Taj complex. The building on the west, to the right of the tomb, is a mosque. Prayers were recited for Mumtaz Mahal here. Prayers are still said here on her death anniversary. And every evening, the namaaz is recited here at sunset. The architectural forms of the mosque echo the elements used in the tomb, but in red sandstone with marble inlay which provides a difference of texture and visual context.

Architecturally balancing the red sandstone mosque is the guest house or mehmankhana on the east, to the left of the tomb. Here too, red sandstone with marble inlay has been used most effectively to provide a foil to the white of the tomb. Careful geometric proportions and spacing bestow a sense of completeness and order to the whole.

When these buildings were in use, the Mehmankhana must have bustled with activity as people gathered to observe the anniversary of Mumtaz Mahal's death. The Mehmankhana would have been furnished with carpets and curtains, awnings and hangings. The glint of copper vessels and the glow of torches and lamps would have illuminated the building as the chatter of voices rose from within the high ceilinged spaces. The rough texture of the sandstone and the intensity of the dusky red stone would have served as a backdrop for the richly woven rugs and textiles that were used against it. We can get an idea of the sumptuousness and variety of furnishings that were used in Mughal buildings from the miniature paintings of the period. There were awnings and hangings, decorative screens and cushions of various kinds, exquisite carpets and floor coverings. Against the rich colours of all these materials, would have been the equally varied textures of the garments and jewels worn by the noblemen of the court. When the mehmankhana was in use it would have been filled with deep toned, jewel- coloured fabrics and garments, all set off by the red stone of which it is built.

On the other side, at the mosque, the activity would have been orderly and disciplined, as befits a place of worship. And yet here, too, the glow of rich textiles and the glitter of jewellery would have filled the space with life and colour. Visualized from the gateway, one may imagine how one offset the other, just as the buildings do, varied in usage but identical in architectural conception, one mirroring the other in perfect symmetry.

The identity of the architect or architects who actually conceptualized and built the Taj remains steeped in controversy. Every now and then the subject is revived and there is a flurry of articles in journals and newspapers, with theories flowing in various directions. Architects from India, Europe and Iran are often mentioned as the 'real' individual who provided the idea and created the form. There is no final answer to this dispute. It would seem that the form had many progenitors over the years, for individual architectural elements may be traced back to the previous reigns. The use of white marble inlay in sandstone at Sikandra, Akbar's tomb, and the tomb of Humayun before that, provide precursors to forms that were perfected at the Taj. The tomb that Nur Jahan built for her father, Itmad-ud-Daulah, used marble inlaid with semi-precious stone with such exquisitely beautiful craftsmanship that it is sometimes said to rival the Taj in sheer decorative splendour. All these elements of design and decoration were already in the air, so to speak. They came into focus,and were brought to perfection in form and workmanship in the Taj. It was, in that sense, a logical heir to all that had gone before.

The names of two master craftsmen who supervised the construction are known with some certainty; Mir Abdul Karim and Makramat Khan are names that are mentioned in the records of the period. The name of the calligrapher has also come down to us across the years. Amanat Khan was originally from Iraq and had already made a name for himself in the reign of Jahangir. His skill was recognised by Shah Jahan and we can see for ourselves how masterly a calligrapher he must have been.

The dome was built under the supervision of another expert. Ismail Afandi was the product of the Ottoman School and came from Turkey. Ustad Isa, as Afandi came to be known, brought his knowledge of designing domes to the service of the emperor of Hindustan.

Similarly we know that the team of inlay workers was led by a man called Chiranji Lal from Delhi. From the evidence of a panel of marble pietra dura at the Red Fort in Delhi, some scholars have suggested that the inlay work may have been carried out under the supervision of an Italian specialist. This has generated a great deal of controversy. There is a panel of unmistakably Florentine pietra dura in the Diwn-i- Am in the Red Fort at New Delhi. This delicately worked inlay, featuring Orpheus and his lute is likely to have been imported as a panel and inserted into the wall.

V.A. Smith, in his *History of Fine Art in India and Ceylon,* wrote, "The Florentine pietra-dura inlay, a revival of the ancient Roman opus sectile, first appears according to Major Cole in the Fabbrica Ducab built by Ferdinand I, Grand Duke of Tuscany in 1558. The earliest certain Indian examples being considerably later in date and identical in technique, a strong presumption arises that the art must have been introduced into India from Italy."

However, in his book *The Industrial Arts of India,* Sir George C.M. Birdwood maintained that Austin de Bordeaux introduced pietra dura at the Taj and while Florentine in origin and style the "designs have a thoroughly local character of their own and . . . adhere strictly to the principles and methods of Indian ornamentation."

B. Havell, in *A Handbook to Agra and the Taj,* writes "on technical grounds it is difficult to understand why a French goldsmith and jeweller should be made responsible for inlaid stone work similar in technique but

totally different in design to Florentine pietra-dura."
In his authoritative *Indian Architecture,* Volume I, Percy Brown also agreed that the plaque at the Red Fort was imported from Florence.

As with other scholarly debates, this one is likely to continue. However, it seems clear that although certain artefacts imported from the West, such as the panel featuring Orpheus, were sometimes incorporated within individual spaces, the inlay work that was used so beautifully in the buildings of this period was purely local in design and character, even if the original technique was not.

Other controversies have erupted on whether there were other European experts involved in the architectural conception of the monument. This is also debated from time to time. However, it seems to have little basis in any records or in the style of the building itself.
Sir John Marshal, writing in the Annual Report of the Archaeological Survey of India in 1904-5 says "The Taj is typical in every feature of the spirit of the Orient, of which it is perhaps the highest expression and above all of the Imperial spirit of the age of Shah Jahan, when the keynotes of art were graceful simplicity and elegance and when marble was everywhere taking the place of coarser materials. . .It is inconceivable that a European, like Veronco, imbued as he must have been with the traditions of the Renaissance, could have so completely divested himself of those traditions and could have entered so intimately into the spirit of an alien style as to create not only a masterpiece in that style but one that is true to it in every essential detail."

The Taj is the most celebrated of Shah Jahan's buildings; a readily recognisable symbol of India. However, it was only one of many magnificent architectural creations built under the direction of this great monarch. In Agra, he inherited a fort and palaces built by his grandfather in red sandstone in the style that has come to known as Akbari. He rebuilt a large number of these within Agra Fort, changing the entire look of the complex with his more delicate structures in marble. The richer, more refined quality of the marble, the finer detailing of the carving and marble screens or jaalis, the more opulent appearance of the varieties of semi-precious stone in the pietra dura, the splendid domes and pavilions were all a reflection of the greater grandeur of Shah Jahan's court.

Mughal power, prestige and wealth reached a highwater mark during Shah Jahan's reign. It found expression in all the arts. It may be seen in fascinating detail in the miniatures of this period, which overwhelm the viewer with the opulence of the court and its occupants. A more enduring and accessible expression is to be seen in the architecture of the period, not only in the city of Agra but also in Shahjahanabad in Delhi, the capital that Emperor Shah Jahan built, possibly because Agra was becoming too crowded. Whatever the reason for the shift of capital, the fact remains that the Mughal court moved to the site of present-day Delhi. Here, Shah Jahan built an entirely new city as an architectural expression of his might. In this he was following the example of his grandfather, Akbar, who had built a new capital at Fatehpur Sikri. However, while Fatehpur Sikri was later abandoned and the court returned to Agra, Shahjahanabad remained the capital of the Mughals for the rest of their rule.

While the Taj was being built, the foundations were being laid for the new capital at Delhi, and in the latter half of his reign, Shah Jahan built the city that was to cement and expand his reputation as a patron of architecture. For all the forms and architectural elements that were set into motion during the building of the Taj and the buildings that he created within the Agra Fort, were to come to fruition in the magnificent Red Fort in Delhi and at the elegantly proportioned Jama Masjid that came up in front of the fort. Here, all the experience of building within an existing fort and in creating the world's most beautiful monument were put to use in the designing of a brand new city. At Delhi, Shah Jahan's work came to full flower and arrived at a sense of maturity and dignity. If the Taj Mahal has come to symbolise passionate love, the city of Shahjahanabad proclaimed the might and wealth of a powerful monarch.

The period of splendour lasted until 1658. During this time, Shah Jahan was undisputed ruler of an extensive and powerful empire, with the wealth and talent at his disposal to transform all his dreams into mortar and stone. However, the clouds were beginning to gather. Drawn by reports of the fabulous riches of the Mughal empire, European traders and adventurers had begun to arrive on the coast, seeking a foothold in this fabled land. And, closer to home, the disputes over succession were on the boil again. Of his sons, Shah Jahan favoured Dara Shukoh, who had what we would now call a 'liberal' viewpoint. This alarmed some of the more orthodox interests at the court and, in the intrigues and conflict that ensued, the emperor's less favoured son, Aurangzeb, who had spent many years away from the court in military campaigns in the Deccan, returned to the north, deposed Shah Jahan and, taking him prisoner, declared himself Emperor.

Shah Jahan was incarcerated in the royal apartments at the Agra Fort, from where, perhaps, he had first dreamt of the Taj. Here, it is said, he spent the remaining eight years of his life gazing out across the river at the masterpiece that he had built. Today, visitors to the Fort may share the emperor's last view of his most beautiful building, which shimmers like a mirage across the landscape, ethereal, seemingly composed of the clouds that sometimes gather in the wide blue skies above it.

HOW OTHERS HAVE VIEWED THE TAJ

'Ek bindu noyan neer jal kaler kapol-tale subhra samujjal e-Taj Mahal ....'

''Only let this one tear-drop,
this Taj Mahal glisten spotlessly bright
on the cheek of Time for ever and ever...''
.... Oh King, you sought to harm time
with the magic of beauty and weave a garland
that would blind formless death with deathless form...
This mausoleum stands still and unmoving in its place.
Here on this dusty earth, it keeps death tenderly covered
in the shroud of memory.''

– Rabindranath Tagore

''The Taj Mahal had better claim to count among the wonders of the world than the shapeless masses of the pyramids of Egypt.''

– Francois Bernier

''... Most gorgeous and magnificent mausoleum under the heavens. Those who have admired all that remains of Grecian or Roman art have not seen anything by which a comparison could be instituted or a resemblance conveyed.''

– Major Archer

''It is a thought, an idea–a conception of tenderness–a sigh of eternal devotion and heroic love... well was it said to me by one who loves not India or her races—"If the people of this land really built the Taj, the sooner we English leave the country the better. We have no business to live here and claim to be their masters."

– W.H. Russell

''Materialized vision of loveliness."

– Percy Brown

''So pure, so gloriously perfect did it appear that I almost feared to approach it lest the charm should be broken."

– Bayard Taylor

''Not Architecture! As all others are
But the proud passion of an Emperor's love
Wrought into living stone, which gleams and soars
With body of beauty, shining soul and thought as when some face
Divinely fair unveils before our eyes
Some women beautiful unspeakably–
And the blood quickens and the spirit leaps
And the will to worship bends the half yielded knees
While breath forgets to breathe.
So is the Taj''

– Sir Edwin Arnold

''The Taj was meant to be feminine. The whole conception and every line of it expresses the intention of the designers. It is Mumtaz herself, radiant in her youthful beauty... or rather, we should say, it conveys a more abstract

thought, it is India's tribute to the grace of Indian womanhood, the Venus de Milo of the East."

– E.B. Havell

"The minarets of the Taj are the ugliest structures erected by human hands."

– Aldous Huxley

".... The ivory gate through which all good dreams pass ...."

– Rudyard Kipling

"I cannot tell you what I think (of the Taj) for I know not how to criticize such a building. But I can tell you what I feel. I would die tomorrow to have such another over me."

– Wife of Major W.H. Sleeman

"The central dome of the Taj is rising like some vast exhalation into the air and on the other side the red ramparts of the Fort stand like crimson barricades against the sky. If I had never done anything else in India, I have written my name here, and the letters are a living joy."

– Lord Curzon

USE ME
कूड़ा - पात्र

सूचना
इस स्थान से आगे फोटो
मना है।
PHOTOGRAPHY IS PROHIBITED
BEYOND THIS POINT

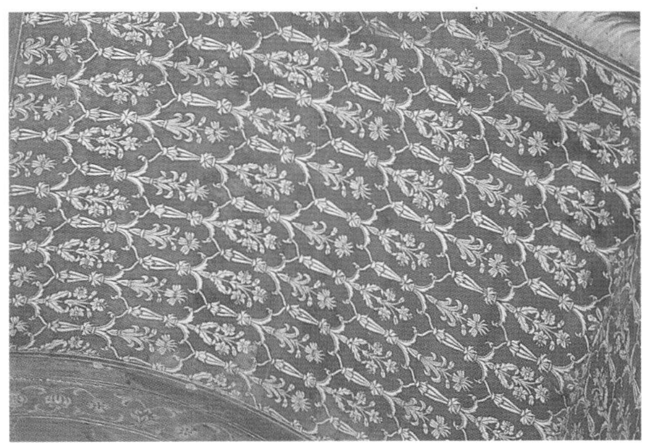

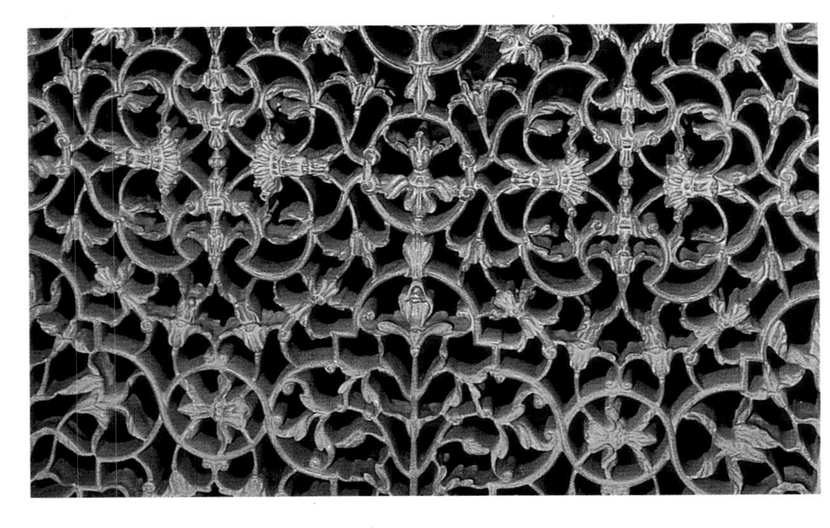

Emperor Shah Jahan always approached the Taj from the river. In the pages that follow, we view this magnificent monument from the Emperor's vantage point. Shah Jahan first identified the site for the Taj Mahal from his palace on the ramparts of Agra Fort. Nestled within a curve of the river, glimmering upon the horizon, set apart from the city, suspended between the bustle of an imperial capital and the glories of nature, the site would have been appropriate in every sense of the word.

Later, when the Taj was complete, the Emperor would travel down the river, approaching his masterpiece gradually. Even today, the most ethereal views of the Taj are to be found from the banks of the Yamuna. The interplay of light and water against the marble creates a gently changing mood, making each image quite unique.

Mughal Agra

Agra witnessed a glorious era of immense wealth, unparalleled enterprise and artistic talent in a period stretching over 100 years from the reign of Babur to that of ShahJahan. Babur, during his brief but eventful rule, built Rambagh, the first Persian charbagh with symmetrical pathways, fountains and running water . His grandson Akbar's first important architectural venture was the strong and majestic Agra Fort built from 1565 onwards. The crescent shaped red sandstone edifice with fortified walls, spans the history of three generations of Mughal dynasty from Akbar to Jahangir and finally ShahJahan. In contrast to its rough exterior, the huge impregnable citadel with beautiful palaces, courts, mosques and gardens, remains an embodiment of Mughal power and prestige.

Akbar also raised another magnificent city, 37 km west of Agra, in the year 1571, as a mark of gratitude for the venerated Sufi saint Sheikh Salim Chisti who had correctly prophecised the birth of his heir. Chiselled entirely from the red sandstone of the rocky ridge, this sprawling and airy complex comprises the famous Bulund Darwaza, Salim Chisti's marble tomb, Jama Masjid, Diwan-i-am, Diwan-i-khas, Daulat Khana or the imperial palace, the intriguing Panch Mahal, several pavilions, gardens and other edifices. This epic in sandstone which was the cultural and commercial centre for 15 years while Agra remained a military stronghold, today stands deserted and desolate, it's ruins echoing the tales and fables of the life and times of one of the greatest monarchs of India.

Akbar's mausoleum at Sikandra, 8km from Agra, exemplifies the unmistakable elegant style of the emperor it so proudly commemorates. The five tiered pyramidal garden tomb, begun by Akbar himself and completed by his son Jahangir in 1613, demonstrates as in all the other monuments built by him, a very fine synthesis of Hindu and Muslim architecture and also emphasises the change from Akbar's strong and resilient style to Jahangir's delicate and aesthetic techniques in building.

Jahangir's wife Nur Jahan built in 1622 another splendid garden tomb,4km to the north of Taj Mahal, in the memory of her father Mirza Ghiyas Beg . An important minister in Jahangir's court, he was bestowed with the title of Itimad-ud-daullah, meaning the pillar of the state. His jewel like tomb is a fascinating combination of translucent white marble, coloured mosaic, precious stones, inlay and lattice work instead of the conventional red sandstone. The evolution of Mughal architecture finally reached its zenith in the pure, perfect and grandiose Taj Mahal that till today defies an apt description.

The glorious days of Agra which resembles any other urban city today were over long ago, but for every visitor and connoisseur of art, this historic city with a rich legacy of art and architecture shall always remain synonymous with magnificence and grandeur.

Photo Captions

Page 1	The monumental gateway through which present day visitors approach the Taj.
Page 2-3	The reflecting pool adds another dimension to the architecture of the monument.
Page 4-5	On a misty winter morning the view from a village across the river is shrouded in mystery.
Page 6-7	The exterior of the monument is adorned with inlay relief sculptures and screens in geometric, floral and calligraphic designs.
Page 8-9	Emperor Shah Jahan always travelled to the Taj by boat, along the river Yamuna.
Page 10	From whichever angle you see, Taj is harmoniously balanced.
Page 30	The marble dados are an exceptionally gorgeous feature of the building.
Page 31-32	Seen from the air, the perfect symmetry of the complex is
33	wonderfully clear.
Page 34-35	Even from outside, the dome of the Taj seems like a fragile bubble resting on the structure.
Page 36-37	The massive red sandstone gateway to the Taj is decorated with floral and calligraphic inlay motifs and surmounted by a row of chhatris.
Page 38-39	At dawn, the Taj has a quiet sense of mystery.
Page 40-41	From the top of the entrance gateway, Taj appears like a jewel in the centre of a geometrically precise charbagh garden.
Page 42-43	Even subsidiary buildings such as the gateway, have been planned down to the last detail.
Page 44-45	Taj appears illusory on a misty winter morning.Taj is magnificent from every conceivable angle.
Page 46-47	Visitors throng the grounds, especially in winter.
Page 48-49	The Taj inspires a contemplative response.
Page 50-51	People come to the Taj from every part of India, and indeed the world.
Page 52-53	The Taj has become a universally recognisable symbol of India.
Page 54-55	The play of light against marble gives the structure a new look at each time of the day.
Page 56-57	In the clear light of the day, the decorative details come into their own.
Page 58-59	The pool symbolsis purity.
Page 60-61	Few first time visitors are prepared for the sheer size of the monument.
Page 62-63	The pristine white marble of the Taj makes a perfect foil to the changing colours of the seasonal foliage and flowers.
Page 64	The reflecting pool adds another dimension to the architecture of the Taj.
Page 65	One needs to pause and study the Taj in a quiet frame of mind to appreciate its power.
Page 66-67	The backdrop of the sky and earth anchors the quick silver quality of the marble.
Page 68-69	The dramatic intensity of the perfectly proportioned Taj.
Page 70-71	The beautiful details of the subsidiary domes.
Page 72-73	The smaller domes cluster close to the central dome.
74	
Page 75	Floral and geometric motifs have been harmoniously balanced on the exterior walls of the monument.
Page 76-77	Decorative details on the niches of the external facade.
Page 78	The play of light and shade against the marble adds to the beauty of the monument.
Page 79	The perfectly proportioned slender minarets.
Page 80-81	Each element of the monument including the garden has been meticulously planned.
Page 82-83	The many different styles of arches within the complex.
Page 84-85	A large number of people gather to offer prayers at the mosque beside the Taj on the Friday before the festival of Eid.
Page 86-87	The mosque echoes the decorative details of the Taj, in red sandstone.
Page 88-89	Decorative elements give the mosque a sense of beauty all its own.
Page 90-91	Inlay relief carving, painting and enamelling are some of the techniques used to adorn the mosque.
Page 92-93	A large number of people offering prayers at the mosque besides the Taj.
Page 94-95	Shifting light and shade create a constant sense of change.
Page 96-97	The reflecting pool.
Page 98-99	The monsoon clouds provide a sense of drama.
Page 100-101	The Taj is astonishingly responsive to minor variations of light.
Page 102-103	Perfect symmetry, regardless of the direction one approaches.
Page 104-105	Four slender minarets frame the central structure.
Page 106-107	Each decorative element has been carefully planned and meticulously executed.
Page 108-109	The finials seem to lift the building towards the sky.
Page 110-111	Floral and geometric motifs have been harmoniously balanced.
Page 112-113	An amazing array of forms.
Page 114-115	The subsidiary domes and pilasters enhance the beauty of the central dome.
Page 116-117	A wide range of semi-precious stones have been used in the inlay work.
Page 118-119	The perfectly proportioned minarets.
Page 120-121	The dome soars up to meet the sky.
Page 122-123	The gently swelling dome lifts the entire structure.
Page 124-125	Each decorative detail is exquisitely executed.
Page 126-127	The geometric, floral and calligraphic decorations at the Taj.
Page 128-129	An amazing range of decorative details at the Taj.
Page 130-131	The cenotaphs lie directly above the actual graves.
Page 132	Delicately carved stone screens.
Page 133	Decorated in fine pietra dura work, the cenotaphs seem like a pair of jewelled